D1413207

Welcome to the Disney Learning Programme!

Sharing a book with your child is the perfect opportunity to cuddle and enjoy the reading experience together. Research has shown that reading aloud with your child is one of the most important ways to prepare them for success as a reader. When you share books with each other, you help strengthen your child's reading and vocabulary skills as well as stimulate their curiosity, imagination and enthusiasm for reading.

In this book, Mr. Potato Head shows Rex and Woody how to juggle. But Rex only has tiny arms. How will he be able to juggle? You can enhance the reading experience by talking to your child about their own experiences of learning a new skill. What did they learn? Who taught them? Children find it easier to understand what they read when they can connect it with their own personal experiences.

Children learn in different ways and at different speeds, but they all require a supportive environment to nurture a lifelong love of books, reading and learning. The *Adventures in Reading* books are carefully levelled to present new challenges to developing readers. They are filled with familiar and fun characters from the wonderful world of Disney to make the learning experience comfortable, positive and enjoyable.

Enjoy your reading adventure together!

Scholastic Children's Books
Euston House,
24 Eversholt Street,
London NW1 1DB, UK

A division of Scholastic Ltd
London • New York • Toronto • Sydney • Auckland
Mexico City • New Delhi • Hong Kong

This book was first published in the UK by Parragon in 2012.
This edition published in the UK by Scholastic Ltd in 2015.

ISBN 978 1 4071 6303 1

Printed in Malaysia

2 4 6 8 10 9 7 5 3 1

Papers used by Scholastic Children's Books are made from woods grown in sustainable forests.

www.scholastic.co.uk

Disney · PIXAR

TOY STORY

LEVEL 3

DISNEY LEARNING

Rex Tries to Juggle

ADVENTURES IN READING

By Lisa Ann Marsoli

Illustrated by Character Building Studio
and the Disney Storybook Artists

Andy and his friends were playing with Andy's toys.

'Go fetch, Slinky!' Andy attached Woody's lasso to Slinky's bone. He threw the bone. He used the lasso to bring it back. It looked like Slinky had brought the bone back!

Andy's mum was downstairs. She called
Andy and his friends.

'Who wants cookies and milk?'
she asked.

'We do!' cried Andy and his friends.
They ran downstairs to eat their snack.

The coast was clear! Woody and the other toys came out to play.

'Let's play baseball!' said Mr. Potato Head. They played with a marble and a pencil. But Hamm was afraid he would get hit by the ball.

'Hamm is afraid,' said Bo Peep. 'Let's
do something else.'

Buzz and Mr. Potato Head began to
play cards.

'Come on, gang,' said Woody. 'Let's do
something we can all enjoy.'

Mr. Potato Head pulled off his nose and ears. He started to juggle. His nose and ears spun over his head. Everyone was excited.

'I didn't know you could juggle,' said Woody.

'I am the best juggler in the toy box,' said Mr. Potato Head.

Rex clapped his little hands. He wanted to juggle too!

'Can you teach me how to juggle?' he asked Mr. Potato Head.

Mr. Potato Head looked at Rex's little arms. He didn't think Rex would be able to juggle very well. But Rex was his friend. Mr. Potato Head decided to try and teach him.

'You must be very careful,' said Mr. Potato Head. 'At first, you will have to go slowly. When you know how to juggle, you can go faster.' He threw his nose and ears over to Rex.

'I'm ready!' cried Rex.

'Now,' said Mr. Potato Head. 'Count to three, and we will start.'

'One, two, three!' Rex shouted. He threw the nose and ears into the air.

One, two, three. The nose and ears went out of the window.

'Oh, no!' cried Rex.

The toys ran to the window and looked down. The nose and ears were now in Andy's garden. They were lying in the grass.

Mr. Potato Head was very cross.
'Come and find me when you get them back,' he said. He went away to play with Snake.

'We have to help Rex,' said Woody. 'How can we get the nose and ears back?'

Hamm picked up some cloth.

'I have an idea,' he said. 'I could float down using this.'

Woody thought about it.

'That will get you down,' he said. 'But how will you get back up?'

Buzz picked up a big, blue ball.

'I have an idea,' he said. 'I can bounce down on this.'

'That will get you down,' said Woody. 'But how will you get back up? The ball won't bounce that high.'

Rex picked up some sticky darts.

'I have an idea,' he said. 'I can climb down on these.'

'This house is made of bricks,' Woody said. 'The darts won't stick to bricks.'

Woody looked at the piece of cloth. He looked at the ball and the darts. He remembered how Andy and his friends had played fetch with Slinky.

'I have an idea!' he said to Hamm.

'First, tie the cloth to my lasso. Then, tape the darts to the ball,' he told Rex. 'Last, loop the lasso around Hamm,' he told Buzz.

The lasso was tied around the cloth. Hamm held onto the lasso. Then Buzz held onto Hamm. Lastly, Rex held onto Buzz. They had made a chain!

Woody sat in the cloth. It was like a swing! Then he sat on the edge of the windowsill. He held onto the ball. 'Hold on tight!' he shouted. He swung out of the window!

Hamm held the lasso tightly. Woody slowly went down to the garden.

'Oh, no!' said Hamm, as he looked below. 'The lasso isn't long enough. Woody won't reach the ground.'

Woody looked down. He saw Mr. Potato Head's nose and ears. They were just below the ball.

Woody knew he could get them. He had to throw the ball just right.

Woody threw the ball to the ground. BOUNCE! Up came Mr. Potato Head's nose. BOUNCE! Up came Mr. Potato Head's left ear. BOUNCE! Up came Mr. Potato Head's right ear.

'I have them all!' Woody shouted. 'Pull me up!'

Hamm pulled the lasso. Buzz pulled Hamm. Rex pulled Buzz. Up came Woody!

'We did it!' shouted Woody. 'Good work, everyone.'

Hamm took Mr. Potato Head's nose. Rex took Mr. Potato Head's ears. Buzz helped Woody get back inside.

Rex went over to Mr. Potato Head. He gave Mr. Potato Head back his ears and his nose.

'Good job!' said Mr. Potato Head. 'Thank you for getting my ears and nose back.' He put them back in his head.

Suddenly, POP! Out fell Mr. Potato Head's eye!

'Oh, Mr. Potato Head!' said Bo Peep. She laughed. 'You really must be more careful with your face!' She gave him back his eye.

'We can't juggle with Mr. Potato Head's face any more,' Woody said. 'It's too dangerous.' He saw Snake playing with some orange ping-pong balls. 'Can you teach us to juggle using these?' he asked Mr. Potato Head.

'Of course,' said Mr. Potato Head.

Mr. Potato Head showed Rex first. The orange balls were easy to hold. Rex could use his little arms. He listened carefully to Mr. Potato Head. He started to go slowly. In no time at all, Rex was juggling!

Rex threw the balls over to Buzz
and Hamm.

'You try next,' he said. Buzz picked
up a ball. Hamm picked up a ball.

'I'm not sure,' said Buzz. 'Maybe
Woody should go next.'

Woody picked up the ping-pong balls.

'You must be very careful,' said Mr. Potato Head. 'At first, you will have to go slowly. When you learn how to juggle, you can go faster.'

'I'm ready!' cried Woody. 'One, two, three!'

Oh, no!